"Agape at the grotesque monstrosity of love and the complex fragility of human emotions, Swain expertly weaves a rich tapestry of unusual poetic flair combined with myriad emotional and nature related intersecting symbolic patterns of implied sublimity."

—The Neglected Ratio

"The reader falls in love with the author."

—Elizabeth Mobley

"John Swain's *Ring the Sycamore Sky* can be described in terms of what light would do to the earth if there was no night to bestow on it.

His words envision a sacred nature where animals and the living creatures beyond the piles of raw vegetation of the wild can possess or address the mystery of life commanded by different sources of light, among which, love is the most sought after."

—Marlena Bontas

Copyright © 2014 John Swain

All rights reserved. This book or any portion thereof
may not be reproduced or used in any manner whatsoever
without the express written permission of the publisher.

Cover design & layout by Stephanie Bryant Anderson
Cover photo by Rebecca Miller

Ring the Sycamore Sky

John Swain

Printed in the United States of America
First Printing, 2014
ISBN 13: 978-0-9915538-4-6

Red Paint Hill Publishing
Clarksville, TN 37040
www.redpainthill.com

A portion of the proceeds will go to The Autism Foundation of TN

Ring the Sycamore Sky

John Swain

Contents

Acknowledgments

Light is Altar /17
Clifty Falls /18
The Creek Continues /19
The Underside of a Leaf /20
Rain on the Gates /21
Indwelling /22
The Embankment /23
Catamaran /24
Dedication /25
For the Reign Succeeding /26
Balm /27
Off Harmon's Ferry /28
The Courtyard /29
Wake /30
Sandspit /31
The Winnowing /32
Fruit of the Orchard /33
A Gathering /34
The Balcony /35
Wreath /36
1937 /37
Tranquility of Nails /38
Below Flowering Trees /39
Cathedral Rock /40
The Closest Sea Bell /41
Ringbone /42
The Only Books /43
Sunday /44
Wearied of Rest /45

Prominences/46
Set Apart Before the World Was Made/47
The Cliff Swallows Glow /48
On the Dune/49
Rookery/ 50
Suddenly the Light/ 51
Muscatatuck /52
Rivulets/ 53
The Hawk Departed/ 54
Osprey Embathed/ 55
Half Moon Lake/ 56
The Understory/ 57
The Shine Overhead/58
Auspice of the Pines/ 59
Certainty and Knowing/ 60
The Estuary/ 61
White Shell Point /62
One Day's Warmth /63
Ambergris Lantern /64
A Weeping Tree /65
Genevieve's Song /66
On the Fallow /67
The Clover Bell /68
Everything Shines /69
Hermitage /70
Cattails/71
Fragments of Calendars /72
The Locust Post /73
Given Weeping Willows /74
A Chandelier Shatters /75
In the Loess /76
Tresses of Feathers /77
Clover on the Levee /78
Replenishing /79

White Cloth /80
Kindling /81
On the Ferns /82
Through Blue Indiangrass /83
Lightship /84
The Fallen Door /85
Harvest Sky Diadem /86
Under Sumac /87
Chant /88
Canebrake /89
Against the Gloaming /90
The Offered Garments /91
Binding of Branches /92
Coronations /93
Preparation of the Ashes /94
Enough of the Plenty /95
Invocation on the Gravel /96
Medallion on the Banks /97
The Trampled Grasses /98
The Blackwater /99
Interlace /100
Thundersnow /101
Blood River, Kentucky /102
The Harrow Succors /103
Over the Alder Grove /104
The Bay Dreamt /105
Land Between the Lakes /106
The Blue Corridor /107
The Railing /108
Where Valleys Fell /109
Rose Window /110
Ladder of Arrows /111
Scattering of Migrations /112
The Shelter Wood /113

Queen Anne's Lace /114
Sun Purified /115
Epitaph Seven Years Past /116

Biography

Acknowledgments

Amarillo Bay, Asphodel Madness, Blue Lake Review, Calliope Nerve Media, Cherry Blossom Review, Clockwise Cat, Counterexample Poetics, Crisis Chronicles Press, dead paper, ditch, erbacce press, Flutter Press, Full of Crow Press, Gloom Cupboard, green panda press, Heavy Bear, Ink Sweat & Tears, Journal of Truth and Consequence, Kleft Jaw, LEO Weekly, Litsnack, Lustre Magazine, Menagerie, Medusa's Kitchen, New Mirage Journal, Opium Poetry 2.0, Poetry & Writing Magazine, Raven Images, Red Fez, Red Poppy, Rust and Moth, Shoots and Vines, Thunderclap Press, Up the Staircase Quarterly, Word Catalyst Magazine.

Light is Altar

I bury a throne in your shoulder
as swaying horses glisten on the hill,
black gallops shatter the limestone roll,
the splendor of hooves stills the bewilder
of this leaving world enrobed with snow.
And since the light is altar,
you drink from the wingbone of an eagle,
we creatures shield into the bare earth,
no longer held in harm or disquiet.

Clifty Falls

Salve of light kaleidoscopic through maples
as the day slowly drifts behind the red ridge,
the focused sun travels in tumbled columns
pressing pathways for us between the branches,
Esther bounds like an adventuress before me.
The creek bed is dry, its stones loose underfoot,
pools collect at turns and trap the tiny fish,
walls of blue rock like illuminated book sky,
I take a scraping away to flood my unborn mind.
Incipient drippings were waterfalls in spring,
now nourish the ferns hanging like a girl's braid.
The clarity of water is a palace in my hands,
enter in like a procession of rope dancers.
The smoke of deer emanates from a strange hearth
as we then ascend a staircase of exposed roots.

The Creek Continues

Summer afield between curtains of rain,
our faces blurred but the semblance did not kiss,
breath caused the trembling of violets.
And the quiet then is silver radiance,
the sky she flatters fairly to remember
while the creek continues under willows.
We lay unending in the charity of days,
omens glisten like seeds in the tall grass,
like sleep she undoes the sun's magnificence.
Hopeless to find another room of air,
she will restore the puddle stones to agate
and jewel the space of disappearing walls.

The Underside of a Leaf

Stained glass shimmers in open vine tangles
beneath the gentle folding of the dandelion hill,
caterpillar sacs illumine branches like lanterns.
The breeze made obeisance before green royalty,
azure tapestries furled back into stratus clouds
and the sky opens again its banners like lips.
The sycamore trees cannot teach us their language,
though slow to learn, I translate with hands
and accept the mysteries of beauty with gratitude.
This circle of moths is our approximate future,
cuttings of bitter gourd will sustain us tonight,
I wear your silver necklace buried in my wrists.

Rain on the Gates

The ironwork bends into its vined ornament
as the porch collapses like a box of rain,
water fills the candle jars black with ash.
In the weeds and dirt I found a heavy bell
that called my mother home from her playing,
droplets on the rust ran with dried blood.
The day lies grey on flowering cherry trees,
petals lost to wind will blanket the ground,
sunlight come weld me to this feather bed.
Inside these warming arms like ringing voices,
I will return to a birth by simply waking,
sky spires extend from the water of our eyes.

Indwelling

Upward where the sandstone juts through split cedar
yellow and red poppies line the mountain road,
light radiates the chapel of its unknown body here.
Rivulets immerse blue caverns beneath the sliding rock,
the refreshing fall carried us through crystal openings
and Daniel laughed in pleasing rings of echoes.
The sky disguised the basin with its tinted reflection
as the sun unlocked its face at the curvature of worlds,
salamanders alternate basking in light and shadow.
The fragrance of iridescent droplets clings to our backs
like an embalming wine overflows,
then the freed water returns to its sepulcher of clouds.

The Embankment

Herons where the diverted channel ponds at the embankment.
Arches of snapped trees hold the herons in their reflection
still as a hieroglyph.
Decomposing leaves in the water produce a bitter humid odor
as bales of painted turtles sun
and then disappear from the sandstone.
Noon poised on the char of clouds
as I looked through the translucent crescent of a redhawk wing
and the palatial sky between us closed for one instant.
Adrift in the billows like a pleasure,
I rested in the bed shade of the beech as the ecstatic
blue presence of a celebrant sealed herself in my shen ring.
The summer sun screamed
like a red-shouldered hawk in wind.

Catamaran

Grey cloud groves disperse among the aviary terraces
where the bones of crushed votive statues melt in the sun,
the burning turquoise drifts against hillsides of lichens
as watchtowers extend from green canopies above the sea.
The day unfurls a flowing sail
and on the shore iguanas climbed the poisonous trees,
bow netting between the hulls held several tan bodies.
The waves pressed against your shoulder like a vault
while the gentlest red coral flowers tore at my belly,
churning blue currents designed arabesque tapestries.
And sunlight only against the azure against boat whiteness,
the water on your skin glowed iridescent as darting fish,
the intoxicating liquors we tasted were nothing but water,
the sail arched again like a leopardess back under tunics.

Dedication

Quicklime covers flower bodies of asphodel
beside the dry meander of the riverbed trail.
As the cobalt light dedicates its reflection
two collectors chiseled to open stone globes
for the quartz revealed like a temple door.
Minerals compress in the expression of mind.
Pillared down from the outcropping enthroned
the drip of a waterfall begins in constant thirst.
I left my tobacco at the base of a dead tree,
a hawk overhead is the crossroad of this valley.

For the Reign Succeeding

Winter crystallized over hazel twigs like a divination
I could never learn to practice,
yellow ribbons of blossoms sweeten the shrouded day.
Scent beneath her arms ennobled our cleanest linens,
the white sheet buried an expanse of grey sky,
which the gyrfalcon reveals like a seer.
Dawn opens itself like a woman's beautiful nakedness
as we swim suspended in pools of lavender air
where the cold sand compressed into red jeweled glass.
The heraldic sea proclaims its language from a spike bed,
a pressed bed of poppies she pleases me to fear.
Then the ships with nets of fish enter the snowy harbor,
I imagine the silver of its mirror left entire
for the emanating glimpse of a tender reign succeeding.

Balm

I heard you gathering skirt pockets of lavender at the fence
like a balm for the thorn distressing this touch at evening
as wind inscribed itself in adoration on your red linen hems.
Stems branch and flower underground as their arteries
color the transparent skin of the sweeping meadow in purple.
We paint each other's eyelids with a tincture
and inhale the solemn fragrance the alembic sun distills.
A sky opens breathing between skies
like a blue morning glory,
I am not sleeping when I listen to this world pierce its aurelia
and scatter black swallowtails from your palms.
Twilight soothes the silhouettes of trees at the forest's edge
while the offering of your own mouth tastes like almond.

Off Harmon's Ferry

The green field's arms reclaimed the abandoned thresher
where bees feed on the nectar of endless clover
as graces of deer bound through wheat toward the stream.
A dead opossum bared its skeleton for the cloud of flies,
turtles muddied the ruts in the gravel after the storm
as landowners leave the snapped timber to rot like a body.
Cattle rush to the poison flesh of wild cherry trees.
A neighbor cut lavender for us to repel the biting insects
though the bramble windswept hills today are impassable,
the wildflowers thrive from the kindness of thorn.
Trees grow downward in the spectral reflection of the lake,
a fallen leaf scared the heron to flight as we rested in emblem,
the sun washed over skin between robe lines of blue rain.

The Courtyard

Barbed wire guards the fountains of tiled courtyards.
Pear-sized hummingbirds abandon shrubs of white flowers
in the evening while fruit flies blackened littered rinds.
The sunset spread like a wine stain on the tablecloth,
the sky darkened its vines with clusters of black grapes,
a blond man undressed and ran laughing toward the sea.
Rocks held the moon's reflection while the surf receded,
I siphoned water until the elusive light remained like a pearl.
Frogs echo in the heart chambers of termite-eaten palms,
for a tongue to speak like them I will excavate a bell.

Wake

Salt encrusts the air of morning like a canopic jar
as the sun casts bronze nets over the chopping saltwater.
The sleek body of a shark challenges the body of the hull
until release.
Eventually rain
drops on black water like obsidian glass of opening eyes
while the wind sound conchs over the lips of our bottles.
As the nimbus clouds pass, the sea swallows.
Egrets preen in the reeds on the shore as the tide recedes
like an alabaster terrace drying her most delicate linen.
Wake movements ease into a blue shudder of calmness,
I lounge in the bow until the fisherman calls for me.

Sandspit

A clarion storm bellows like a ram over fossil cliffs
as choirs of high winds vibrate the aching stone basin,
silk threads fall as the chrysalis of air detaches.
After the drifts, spits of land emerge in the river,
the sand of powdered garnet could not support my weight
when the waters receded,
fish scales glisten rotting in the crevice of limestone,
flesh and eyes were picked by vultures,
I left behind my fallen shape as the crater fills with rain.
Men pulled flathead catfish from the river heavy as men.
The flood crest tangled drowned horses in the tops of trees
as the lightning brightens like brass lamps over a bowl
of bitumen incense and fragrant water lilies.
The locks continue to lower barges like a clepsydra.

The Winnowing

Daybreak and the remains of the sky finally knelt
on the blue expanse of its vibrance shining like weaponry,
I cried praises for your heart's warmer lasting.

Skylights color crater pools like a bruise on purple fruit,
we washed our callused hands there
to touch dawn and be clean.
Shade created pale havens on the paths of weathered stones
where the river deposits its rust-wash and corroded barrels.

Juniper trembled in the wind like my lips against cloth,
the intention and circumstance held bright sails to your nape
as your skirts trail the gentlest flow of water like pure idea.

Fruit of the Orchard

Mountain heather extends from fencerows to the setting sun,
the sky suffused with the red fruit of the orchard
as succulent aloes relieve the pain burnt after this witnessing.
Summer opens bells of pears
as the tree becomes full light, light like the clarity of bells
a ribboned woman on horseback is ringing.
The evening does not cool the heavy air
holding pink honeysuckle,
sweat glistens where hair transmits the perfume of her body,
the precious and beautiful vapor inspires an oracle.
Fennel flowers yellow at the breathtaking confluence of rivers
as I cleansed my animal skin with limewater for handwriting.
Arcades of black pumice and vines outline
against the porphyry sky,
I am thankful for the shade our closed eyelids provide.

A Gathering

Sandhill cranes vortex in layers spilling downward,
dry stalks and wheat color the winter field in quiet gold.
The field of deer lies still without fear like Kathleen asleep,
for there are no hunters tonight.
I hope she hears the brass trill of cranes trumpeting
when she is at loom weaving colorful pillows for sale,
they each return the beauty of this world.
I rest in the marsh on the facial disc of a female harrier
as she shivers then now in her cold voice,
which encloses me like a glass hymn.
The sky breaks like porcelain in rain
although I have nothing more to say in my pointed hat.
The scythe wind like a crescent moon prepares the wheat,
the last sheaf cut becomes the maiden of our festival.

The Balcony

River evening as rowboats emptied onto the stones,
I dreamt fragmented from the balcony.
Intoxication and your fragrance of night-blooming jasmine
like delight of interest though
your staggering shadows would rather adorn a floor of topaz.
Reclining onto a green chair,
your gemmed feet smooth as the fruit of anise in my hands.
Fearing gently I lie on my back
beneath the bats gathering insects from the surface of water
as dawn crept to lie beside you in the shallows.

Wreath

I say joy to you,
receive a wreath of hands
and featherbells
for the days
we live without love.
And on this bed of embers
I will not lie in grief
for all the glowing world
within breathes
rain and sleep.

1937

After the flood,
horses float through the trees
captured in the tall branches
like fish nets.

Tranquility of Nails

The sweep of sand
weathers the fossil stone
imperceptibly.
The tortured drift
has come to rest
where the river inscribed
its ineffable testament.
Shards of glass, remnants
imitate the pink wound
of the horizon.
Eagles are nesting,
but no one has seen them.
I dream here
seeking the tranquility of nails,
cast from splintered wood
onto the ground,
bent and useless,
not holding anything.

Below Flowering Trees

Below flowering trees
the tapestry of sun and sky
unravels blue and yellow.
The river reaches upward
becoming breathing air.
Your dreamt eyes flood pear petals
over the spring corridor
like a child
follows after the last bride.
Then I fall sunken in white
like a paper boat
in the pond trees succeed
over ages like a pillar.
Inwardly unredeemed,
I am not pardoned
by own my heart
for choosing surrender,
I will always lie here.
The stone bridge shimmers
where the water presses
its image over our faces
touching on either side
of the surface
like the earth of a grave.

Cathedral Rock

The crystal gleam of leaning palms
darkens the cliff
and blends with the upreaching sea.
A half-sun rides the cresting waves
and slips behind the cathedral rock,
light fires a mandala of arrows
against the sky of blue flowers.
The stones we cast shine like coins,
scuttling red crabs devour papayas
on the moist floor
while the canopy shades dart frogs
and we perspire in a silent ecstasy.
The black streambeds were asleep,
I chased a rattling green kingfisher
into a clearing of freshwater,
its circle blurred a face of light,
you are beautiful
naked facing a bark mask in transformation.
I retrieved this initiate glimpse
through shadowed vine tangles
leading deathward like a nightfall
as serpents devour the moon
of bright yellow birds.

The Closest Sea Bell

The sail carves its ghost
onto a sky of bone.
The closest sea bell falls silent
as wind and current
move in opposite directions.
We find stasis,
then jump into the water
freed like the sea expanding
to myth from itself.
The boat catches sunlight
in the gentle roll over us,
each a pyramid exalting
the changing islands
moving like the quiet body
of a queen in dormition.

Ringbone

Gone you hallow
as snow dust covers the field,
the trod earth fills my mouth
as the sun condemns us rise.

Gone you carry
ash and water to where we slept,
ceremony distills no revelation here,
the house of foundation is broken.

Gone you disenthrone
the learning we took from wind,
crown me as beast and I will tear
us living back from the burial.

The Only Books

Only the shadow of crows on the road,
only the bit plum flesh while we swim,
only the light that outlines our sleeping,
these are the books that I know.

Sunday

Sunday numbed
roses in the dark eye
of a white horse
at the splintered fence
like the weariness
bearing all the days
we pretend to inhabit
like a glimpse
of ourselves.
The sun drifts
to the end beginning
of the world
on a splintered raft.
I am thirsty
you are fountain
in this wasteland
where mountains drown.
Wake me up
before it is dark,
we have guests to welcome
and a meal to prepare.

Wearied of Rest

White poppies will sprout
from your bruised wrists,
sleep in the spring rain,
let fall your red sun dress.
Waken and invent a face,
the water surrounds you
in movement and glimpse
like a given name
until the sky becomes a body
where we drift in all praise.
Touch closer than blood,
breathe in crushed leaves
as to slowly forgive
the undoing of all we aspire.

Prominences

Sun singe, glimmer, then purge,
we taste the burnt ground
where riding people threw coins.

Yet you speak perfect words,
not caring for the meadowlark
in your throat like earth's old voice.

I will pour clean water
for your thirst when all birds light
from where we lay twisting shovels.

Despite the chars of our coupling
you open my side with dry fingers,
allowing the horses to drink.

Set Apart Before the World Was Made

Gale chains embrace horizon like relief
portending a source of new water.
I brought a simple cup to the river
and you kept the signets pressed into wax.
People slept beneath the flood wall
like wolves bound under snow
and in the morning
dawn expended its tithe of starling flocks
to the merlin falcon.
I live in the spaces you had forsaken,
although the light was given first to you,
it is my only guide.
Impermeable stone bowls trap rainwater
with an honest forgiveness
that I could not tell the air or ever receive
after we burned the deer heart and gall
upon a fire of fragrant leaves and branches
in the corner of the room like a forest
set apart a hidden altar to eat of its child.

The Cliff Swallows Glow

Arise and the arch of cliff swallows glows
in metallic blue beneath the winged curve of the stone bridge
where the river lies in emerald.
Every love and all that is known lives in the sun in your eyes
like a rite, then we swim and the waters cleanse
as the afternoon opens like dawn.
Our shadows chase schools of little silver fish
to the fallen trees,
the mirage of you breaks statues
like warm childhoods of light
on the sand where the hypnotic water rejoins
the aching sky forever.
Prism river droplets from your hair disappear onto the ground
I grasped after to stand
in the scatter like a dancer in a pure trance.

On the Dune

Horizon of rain like rutile silk fractures.
On the dune masts of abandoned sailboats clank
and I thought of your hand
as the ocean spread its net of black sapphire.
Owls sounded in the palm scrub
before we climbed to the shoreline,
wine spilled from our mouths as we lapped
at each other in the door of the water
like an erasing.
I tasted the salt like the sea of your body,
the beauty of this world pulsates like dark blood
courses the sky of lightning.

Rookery

Rookery in the snag of fallen trees
as rainwater in the craters returns to sky,
dragonflies depart
beneath a green veil of liquid wings.
I read galleries of tunneling worms
in the driftwood,
hand over hand caresses its sun whitened skin.
Sun on the river floods
like the cut of a red plum,
as the ending light spills
the climbing stones darken.
I still myself trying not too much to hope
for another voice
in illusion of union
to color the air like the herons returning.

Suddenly the Light

Suddenly the light decreed uprising
like a certainty
the blue mountains accepted.
Golden eagle feathers spread
above the shield of the winter valley
like a sage whispering
tidings of distance to his emperor.
Clear rivers fill crystal eyes
with white fire as you climbed
upon my wrist like a hunting bird
and we rested together.
Then like a willow you grew entwined
with the raining light,
its silence makes me stronger,
its brilliance makes you true.

Muscatatuck

The forest fled into meadows of goldenrod
grown endless under moth wings fluttering,
I lift my face to sky hypnotized by azure.
Hawk feathers adorn the fallen beech tree,
I called you dawn cut with pure assurance
like an animal wails.
The pathways flood,
frogs teem emerging from puddles of origin.
Pines incense the remains of a slain deer
we discovered under needles near the creek,
its ribcage spiked upward like a monument,
sun whitened the bones in wines of light.
I hung my own skin to dry from the branch
snapped like antlers of a prince's crown.

Rivulets

Sparrows enliven incarnadine grasses
by the river as birch skin trails the wind
like beaten prayer flags.
I watched the water falling
where hills spilled rivulets over sheer limestone
like a necklace strand.
Cloud shadows mask the silhouettes of trout
like a silver treasure,
all is loved
what I am not,
you do not have to suffer.
Calm as an osprey in my shattered body
and still wanting
steps on the precipice to soften mosses
in the becoming unknown.

The Hawk Departed

Fallow the valley of candles smolders in ember,
reflections of egrets stamp on the molten river
like a skirted girl on an ancient vase.
I crossed the creek of stone into fields of ironweed
whose bells of amethyst clamor like a firmament.
Awed by the touch of trees pulsating after the hawk departed,
my mouth fills with azure as praises form like a sky.

Osprey Embathed

The moving blue water blurs into sky
as the pier extends and then disappears,
fish swim glimmering like silver handwriting
as the sea arches at your caress.
An osprey hovers in stillness of sky and ocean
then falls like pillars
and returns to the spire of a dead tree.
The shadows falling bathe me in forgetting,
a name is called and I do not answer.
The tearing sky and water merge like flight
of our shapes combined
in a burnt mask of sea and wings and claws.

Half Moon Lake

Light before the light
until the light disappears
in winter grasses holding the harrier low
as my ghost in its throat.
I swallowed my wounds
like gathered water
where the rushing stream enters to rest
in Half Moon Lake.
I thrust my hands in the flood path
for stones to hold a skin over me.
The cipher sky adored reborn
every instant of breath
the day distilled
under this crush of longing.

The Understory

Amber shadows recede like a blue sleeve
in the understory
where a tree snake entwined like a vine on a branch.
Presented like a wax tablet,
I memorialized the sunrise with a knife
against the tuber pith of the morning glory,
blood reddens the center of its white flowers.
Sun like plum flesh in our mouths,
daylight dances reflecting your golden jewelry
like the bound of doe and fawn.
Mosses hang from the laked trees in iridescence
like a dogbane leaf beetle feeding on milkweed,
all bodies radiate with light's signature
written on a leaf of skin as dawn
robed your throat like a prothonotary warbler.

The Shine Overhead

Vulture circles shine overhead like an ancient mask
we wear for a face of protection.
The rain of sun drips like nectar encasing the birch,
the falling rain of sun draws the birch trees upward.
Trees expose bitter fruit throbbing in the throats of birds,
mourning doves leave branches for seeds on the ground
as the rotten pods hang like suicides condemned.
Shadows cool the stones which line the excavated hillside
though the burst sun remains in its darkened corridors
like eclipse on the mirror as you glimpse yourself immersed.
And I said nothing in praise or complaint of the day,
maintaining the estrangement from my closest friend.
Black sap bleeds like wine from the punctured trees
as we embrace a carillon of their swaying incantations,
I describe the shade written on your back of palimpsest.

Auspice of the Pines

Outline of blue hills shivers blue as the lake
where water filled the valleys over towns submerged,
the mirrored surface undisturbed by the spiked trees.
The solitude of winter eased into a capsule of sleep
as creek moisture blackened the gold stalks and leaves
where the bones of a fallen deer were carried by dogs.
I am soothed by a sky you remember like a bruise
away over the iron field muddied by the dust of snow,
a horned owl in the naked treetop startles,
its shadow on the path opens like a book of incantations.
The breathing winds incise the body of a row of pines,
the opening cut a blood moon into my palms,
you applied mosses to alleviate the wound
as the hollow trees gleamed a conjuring labyrinth.

Certainty and Knowing

Careless are days
when I mistake
certainty and knowing,
one is sun,
the other is
your arms around me
sleeping.

The Estuary

The estuary pours the river into horizon
where the night herons tower like guards
on the splintered branch of a tree adrift.
Pyramid orchids flower in the moist air
like beads of sweat at the back of your dress
distilling fragrance as this incense burns.
Root galleries enliven the sleeping cicadas,
the movements of sunset amplify their sound.
Tidal currents efface the indigo vestige
of night at the threshold of this charred dream.
We swim in melted armor where sea swallows river
while the changing shore cries like a heresy.

White Shell Point

Gulls circle like a diamond pendant on the spindrift
where the ships move rhythmic as your breathing,
mists of the domed sky veil the curvature of sails.
Frothing white caps moisten the dissolving shore,
serpents of sand grains entwine and chase themselves
as sea oats bent tortured where there are no flowers.
Lightning floats where the enraptured sea collapsed,
a shell in my pocket spiked my thigh like a tooth.
I sought nothing to preserve much as the grist
like salt in our mouths as the darkening light scatters.
Swarms hummed over the dunes past lizard tongues
while another brood emerges from a buried dulcimer.

One Day's Warmth

Tiers of green willows cling to the rock and silt
where coal dust from the river blackens the shore,
skies beguile the correspondence of mutual bodies.
Polished stones of every color soften our fingers
like the shell of a dead turtle preserved,
gulls swirl in chaos where turbines churn the fish.
Raining legions trample the domed ceiling
while I taste bits of grape seeking forgiveness,
with one day's warmth the hillside spasms violet.
Water laps against the escarpment like a pendulum
as shadows paint the length of our tired faces red,
there weathering becomes chrysalis for a moth.

Ambergris Lantern

Winds sweep across the vaults of sea
as dolphins arch a tender omen.
Rune gusts on the surface water writhe
in a dance of possession
while girls chased birds on the sand.
The osprey perched in a dead tree like a shaman.
The saltwater distills this bluest sky
burning like myrrh
as I inhale the treasure of your body's fragrance.
The sea of light burns a glowing lantern
in our stone window,
I dreamt incense smoke to praise your presence,
then the ashes traveled like winged seeds,
lucid as love's idea.

A Weeping Tree

Vanish your name
with oceans breaking
on the rock shore
in semblance of praise.
The room quiets you,
arms twist to conceal
the baring of legs
and breasts and hair
like the knotted vines
on a weeping tree.
I won't pretend for you,
instead I open my ribs
to your teeth, then
we curl like a beast in the sun.

Genevieve's Song

Past the spaces
between chimes ringing,
there is a meadow.
You seem much farther,
rains from your throat
nourish the soil
I crawled out from
to rain upwards
to the place you created.
We worship here anointed
with the marrow of air,
only for you can I sing.

On the Fallow

All grace gave light on the fallow,
its mimic in the cloud shine hides
our shyness with bodies like grain.

And as the redwing blackbirds born
in the touch of inherited earth,
alive our own we are recreated sun.

The Clover Bell

The clover bell blooms
like a haven
for the sun to rest.
Flower candles light
the windy hillside
with butterflies emerging.
I follow the stream
lilting as your neck
arches with dogwoods.
The red clay vibrates
sounding a pulse
in my own veins
where I feel you living.
The bromegrass courses
unfold diaphanous
then we are summoned
to departure or acceptance
as the light illumines
an unseen sovereign,
I give you my trust.

Everything Shines

A handful of river
pours ingots of sun
into a crucible.
I will make coins
from the hammer
of branches
on the anvil of my body.
Willows trees lilt
at the water's edge,
almost embarrassed
of their iridescence
like the shy.
I take a swathe of leaves
against your cheek
to bring you to me.
Burnt clay holds us
in the summer ring
nearing one place
until the gold fall
returns skyward
with all the world
needing its distance
like the dead
beneath a sheet
from our sight
to armor the passing
of this ardor
after everything shines.

Hermitage

The monastery lake
empties itself to the sky
like a nourishing birth
allows the blue changeling
to find its hiding shape.
I removed my shoes
and touched moss on rocks
in the summer forest
where the creek begins.
Farther down the meander
a wood thrush led me
softly past the hermitage,
I would not disturb him,
I will find my own quiet
beneath a sky of sun
as water touches water.

Cattails

Swaying cattails circle
the water of my emergence,
the lady of consolation waits
inside a shelter of branches.
The trellis collects vines
as white wild roses climb
like a tomb bed
of burst light
against the forest green.
The wind shimmers past
the hill of bluebird grass,
the fragrance of painted ladies
colors the day
at the edge of St. Anne's Meadow.
Showers of azure
penetrate the caves
like a wellspring of stone.

Fragments of Calendars

The abandoned chapel collapses
in a puddle of stained glass windows,
the bell tower stairs in the field
lead upward to sky like the mirage
of a mountain.
I bury your dress in a pile of stones
where the acacia tree shades,
light passes through intricate lace
over the missing.
These uncertain hours crumble
like maggots in a leather book spine.
I filled the pond with earth
and pulled splinters,
then I consulted the fragments of calendars
for an auspicious time to plant
your ruin into the land.
Now with the boundaries tilled,
I can see until blue evening,
nightjars sound from the branches,
though my brothers like horses
had fled before the morning.

The Locust Post

A donkey brays
under tumults of the wave-breaking spring sky
as upturned leaves predict the rains
like a seer wheel of six black vulture wings.
The blue pastures emptied and cows lay down
as winds stripped the dogwoods like a flaying.
The fence wires tremble between locust posts
where knotted vines provide the small birds shelter.
I carved an opening in wood to hide my book
of turning hymn images
from the water in a hollow beneath rough bark.
The dead tree gave me different words to speak
in release
when I am pressed like a dark stone point
I found washing my hands in the rising stream.

Given Weeping Willows

The sun scorched hill touched our backs
beneath the golden talons of a closer sky
as the hawk transforms the squirrel into hawk,
taken prey beatifies the saint within you.
Astounded by diffusions through slight leaves,
we gently leaned like the river against its bank
where a willow dipped gilt hems in the stream,
I trembled at the woman your dark eyes made.
Light inscribes its prayer like a vestment
as the wind convinces the limbs to weep,
I live in that day although I never touched you,
we received another world like fire in the trees.

A Chandelier Shatters

Fireflies illumine the field like a chandelier shatters,
the circling trees dripped with the rain in green night,
the stream water flowed with the ashes of mansions.
I stared upward into the lightning like a white tower
and sealed myself in cloister walls of disappearing,
the giving earth accepted the full weight of my steps.
I forgive myself in difficulty like uprooting jasmine,
its fragrance remains on the moisture of leaf and air,
the blades and shovel could do no work in my hands.
Electric moons glowed in the wing body of each insect
as two girls chased each other in anger past the dark buildings
housing the owls above a pile of bones,
I kept myself near the foundation ground
as the buried light awakes in release from our capture.

In the Loess

The wavering field cries its pain to the hill
where the sun lies pierced on jagged rocks,
I followed with the dry earth on my hands
like your skin when the aching winds died
and the night gave silence to ash and bones.
The path opened when I stopped traveling
and dust taught the river its grave stillness,
I scattered the loess ridge that captured me
then mimicked ascension with a totem wing
as the rain sang arising in tree and mullein.

Tresses of Feathers

Osprey wrists pierce my dream
in a trickling pool beneath the dam
as leaning catfish raise their fins
mocking the talon.
Upon a brief touch,
the dead tree strengthens my arm
to forsake this caging mind.
I cup the water running
from tresses of black feathers
and then return the wine to earth.

Clover on the Levee

Clover shines a softening green on the levee.
The river divests itself of the confining banks
and the falls vanish
as the water above flows level with the pool beneath.
The river thrashes with a violent turbulence,
debris of trees and barrels circles in a maelstrom
while the absence of shorebirds is noticeable,
island rocks of egret colonies are now sunken castles.
The green sky of lightning overtakes the prism sky
and I am alone in the chamber,
fountain worms emerge from the saturated ground.
As the evening concludes like a tryst,
the swollen river is pregnant with freak creatures
from the embers of the barges and factories,
I still hear the sky when I slipped from the line
of the shore and went beneath the surface rushing
downriver until a drowned sycamore stilled me
like the arms of a grey swimming angel.

Replenishing

Galleries of green rain-heavy branches
collect echoes of birdsong and thunder.
The liquid earth abandons stones to float
in the blood of light,
I still distance myself from infusion.
The sound of willows brushing clings to wind
like tender violins in a royal chamber,
I took awe from your parted lips.
Centuries of downfall became a quiet lake
in our cupped hands replenishing air.

White Cloth

I purchased white cloth
to lay across the rain
like the tomb of a queen.
Released from the sky,
we delight
in immaterial textures
borne by our gated mind.
Water became our veil
to touch contemplation
like lucid pears dripping
from your summer lips.

Kindling

Cedars perfume the night air
after we snapped branches
and pledged our dress to fire.
We exchanged ourselves in smoke
and learned to be quiet
as wood havens its mourning.
I shiver somehow in your ghost
as warmth approaches darkness.

On the Ferns

Ferns lay like afternoon
beneath the canopy sheet
of wet green trees
as river tides left a pile
of smooth colored stones
on a bed of mud and stone.
I walked through the blue
truth of our capture
like iron brackets holding
the animal rampant
under a sun of teeth.
The sky let its light catch
a feathered hook dangling
from river oak branches
like a bird of prey
come to take
with all the world alone
far below.
I kept what faith was left
for protection
although we are broken
like bones and horses
before the real flames
make fire of the day.

Through Blue Indiangrass

Dawn wavers through blue indiangrass
like an ivory comb
to groom the horses after days of forest
while sun fire struggles to illumine both horizons
as a beast claws outside of its mother.
Light roams indifferent to my patience
like a wild boar pierces
my rib in the form of a gorgon
as water returns to its source of mirrors.
I continue alone, leaving
the gilt tree shade turned like a woman.
I have excised my arms from purpose,
growing to be nothing owed,
provisions were made before I knew
that you were already a home,
the remnants of garments sit in the dust,
broken chairs are now a mountain behind
the servant horses running.

Lightship

Uprooted trees line the beach sullen as a cemetery
as stripped palms fall arranged bare in column monuments,
the crippled oaks twist in agony like an aborted horse
while a nodding lady sleeps trapped inside the winter glass.

An osprey strikes indifferent to winds at the inlet
and then sends its message to the wandering people.

The spiral tower domes the fire of nine thousand candles,
as another year passed, I threw myself into the solstice water,
the ocean's grey blade held the ashen sun aloft
like a lightship unmoored carries the drowned like a pharaoh.

The Fallen Door

Bare after the rain-sky emptied me like a hill
above the blue shale glowing its aura of phantoms
as if it were the actual river we traveled still living.
I crossed the fallen doorway loam and then slept
where it fell to be written by tunneling worms,
hints of your lilac still perfume this bed,
although the stalking furies reveal my trespassing.
I could not silence myself without invoking your mouth,
gnawed bones fill the hollow splintered from tenderness
with a violence I can no longer explain or ignore.
I hoped to find clean breath to rename myself in smoke
and leave my deeds to the burning place,
but this wind from emptiness thrills the abyss
I was and am still becoming.

Harvest Sky Diadem

The ruby moon crept like a pantheress onto the kill
from the ocean horizon we touched while swimming
in the salt waves crashing like a profound intoxication.
Then we tread in the blood trails of her dress
until the light silvered the beach like a necklace string
that you wear in glamour.
The seawater empties into itself before darkness
and I longed to continually rise this harvest sky diadem
above the black expanse where we are severed.
I do not want to leave in return to myself
when the wind travels and the living water opens
into the private iridescence we imagined like a temple
opened to all.
I surrender to the alchemy of this night conquering.

Under Sumac

Island rocks pulsed a skene behind the stage of the lake
for the dancing corn man to hide,
water fell from cups of sumac leaves then returned in steam
like the distillation of spirits,
I inhaled my share freed from all memories and forethought.
Two red-shouldered hawks instilled each sky with a vision,
I basked in the power of their moving and winged reflection
on the surface caught in sunlight like a calendar wheel.
When the mask of birds shattered, my own face had vanished,
I do not belong to either pall.
The blood of wind numbed the hollow passage in my arms
before this sleep releases the drupe to become a sumac tree
like a smokeless candle burning scarlet
for my return to his transfixed possession and answer.

Chant

Thunderheads at the western edge
seem to deepen the river
like the shadows of eagles pressed
onto a gold medallion.
I watch the frogs climbing the hill
as the last flesh of light
leaves behind a rusted chain
to drag a useless wagon filled with sand
in guilt and denial for existing,
now I must wear this painted yoke
without your twisting arms.
The storm rejoices each direction
with chant and benediction
upon the seasons of drought,
the euphoria of lightning deranges,
to be born like a daughter
again in the growing forest,
its forked course snakes like a tree
through my center.

Canebrake

The canebrake bronze
trembling with bittern
in the sun
until horizon of winds
brought a thundering.
I touched my cut arms
to the river I followed
without a holding
on miles of levee
between floods of oak.
I stood in column air
created by two eagles.
I prayed to nothing
for nothing with a voice
of scream and cypress.
I claimed the mistake
that carried me
to this place of waste
which filled my mind
with devouring idols
like approaching rain
upon the sulphur clay
carved another mask
I will try to abandon.

Against the Gloaming

Stillness drifts against the vervain gloaming
while the lithe white falcon kites like a sylph
between pines and cedar taking green anoles.
The flooded canal field burst with gold reeds
as the tall sawgrass kept yesterday's rain alive,
I cooled myself in the shadow of a footbridge.
The moon twists like an empress into our world,
though the day remains upon us with sapphire
hanging from the sky scented with attar rose.
I searched long the brack to find myself here
tied to the cypresses who gave me a secret life
like a woman in marriage presents the jesses
that bind us together like the spine of a bible.
Night slipped onto the marsh as the falcon
returns to the leather of its hidden master's glove.

The Offered Garments

The sun lowered itself onto red fossil sands
where the river made altars upon the offered garments
of all that is left behind like a skin,
I crossed in haste to acquaint myself.
Then the hill arose from rocks and vines,
white morning glories closed around my feet
beneath an osprey burned into a perch
atop a cottonwood clawed by roots into the earth.
Twilight grants relief to the person I am seldom
like dogs emerge from burrows to scavenge
the path illumined by the moon trailing our own light,
I held a weathered limb to stable my ranging.

Binding of Branches

The chasing sky releases its veils of mist
like a cloud of wolves exposing the mountain
to its own birth into wilderness.
Frenzied trees burst like a consort from soil
as green leaves spiral into bronzed rings
ensuring the order of union,
I am tied forever to your binding of branches.
Shrined chimes mimic the height's vibration
I cleared myself to receive
when the winds bred song from emptiness.
Rain became another queen at the peak,
she tore at her breast to strengthen the young.

Coronations

And kindling light clothed only the evening sky
burnt like an offering the eagle ignited in genius,
I felt the feather you wore pulse inside my neck,
the wind-bended trees moaned like a taken deer.
I pressed a knife into stitches and ate all I found
dark in hollowness where the river washes cliffs,
the shelter grew from within my body like a gall.
Then I twisted out onto the ground of your ashes
like a willowing foal.
Night rides the bird on fire over cool black silks
like an heiress whose weight will never touch the earth,
stone became flowers as the shadow ghosted air.

Preparation of the Ashes

Scythes parted the trees before the world opened
and we received clairvoyance from silver vapors,
the bright day colored your face like a cured leaf.
Sun burned a hawk shadow on the dry watershed,
tomorrow morning I will have to dig another well
as breezes twist our scented washings on the line.
Men found enchantment around your linen dress,
so I explained to them your night before the caliph,
only our angel was stoned by the people in town.
With water from a basin you dampened strips of cloth
as I lit lamps like a watcher measuring our distance,
the scars of this undress astounded me with beauty.
We clamor in the kinship of bronzed leaved arms
reminiscent of the wafer and the camphor bewitched,
I wished you would have placed upon my tongue.

Enough of the Plenty

The lake wind hollowed the winter forest,
ashes fell like feathers on the shore of stones
when I raised my face from last week's snow.
The water arose to embrace the rain
like blossom and thorn cross your white arms
where the prying sun marked its sign of goats.
Paths of birds transformed grey air to jewels
and we cannot be the same
after incision of wings divided the world
back to night like the side of a codex queen
meets a candle burning beneath clear glass,
red fire the blood that scorched her true body.
And then the vanishing into the land
like a tracker's footsteps
I followed still trying to find another way.
Torn books warm the bare dwelling floor,
although I seldom allow myself reminiscence,
having taken enough of the plenty.

Invocation on the Gravel

The gravel shone white against the thundercloud
sounding as the abandoned house vanishes
beneath the branching arch of joining sycamores.
The dying corn stalks folded over like a damask,
I held my arms down in these irritant remnants
waiting the year for another gold entrance to rise.
The crows rejoice in their roost at the darkening,
then we will cleanse our vessels together to store
the grains portending the beginning of a new work.
I walked the road to the bronze of the autumn hill,
the wind and rain lifted the gathering stream
as a horse skeleton began to float from the sand,
there is shelter where briars cross its shoulder,
although I know we have our own hiding place.

Medallion on the Banks

Leaves river parallel with the storming river
in grey winds changing from horses to wolf.
I pray someday to fall
like these spirits quicksilver into themselves
and then move effortlessly into each another
joined to the world like a knowing.
The sun cuts like a medallion on the banks,
I take a brightened stone to keep
as the end of journeys continues on the table
sustaining with the true giving of a woman.
I scrape the mud caked on my wading boots
and leave myself like a dog on the threshold.

The Trampled Grasses

When the moon subdues its initial conflagration
and silvers the night like another day to harvest,
the leaves I trampled shone back upwards.
The exposed rock shelves ascend like a pyramid
to the wine chalice of a sky lake,
I drank again and again from its revealing body.
My life before slept preserved in a wrap of furs,
a red pheasant flushed from where I cut my rib,
then a handful of sand became my only companion.
I burned a queen hibiscus and sage to clean myself
and walked across the matted reeds and grasses
to be empty chewing on roots of the dark sky.

The Blackwater

Skeletons of dead trees arose from the blackwater river
like a ghostly host draped in moss beyond the mill pond
and sand hills burrowed by gopher tortoises.
Back along the overgrown magnolia road,
I scoured my hands with a blunt washing stone,
but the owl still speaks in the scar on my palm.
Remaining in the shape of a man against himself,
I wished for the forgiveness that you would give a stranger
and received a silence I misunderstood,
though tomorrow we must eat from our own ribs like bread.
The summer rain washed away your clean white dress
and quieted the dogs to let me sleep eating apples
of red flowers burst like effigies above incense smoke
on the floating dock to rise and fall beneath a knotted rope
as my rest bed trembles on the stems of arrows.

Interlace

Hawks unfurl black tapestries limitless as western sky
as mountains shattered the reflection of sun on water,
my singing ancestors wrapped their throats with halo fire.
The ground of leaves slipped between the white trees
where I tried to rejoin the future of days ever glowing,
but this silence flooded like rivers in a chapel emptiness.
I buried a pocket of coins and feasted on broken bread
as laying stones held the shine
in angles of the ecstatic roof the dead climbed into eyes.
I wear their new skin interlaced with a zodiac bestiary
and drank the voice piercing the wolf to speak my own
as the earth arose from itself and through our growth.

Thundersnow

Reeds and trees in the river shine with ice,
wind in the bridges sounds a mountain hymn
as the grey sky weighs like a pressed stone.
I blurred into the snow as thunder opened
its pulse like a chrysalis
our mother carried across the tidal waters.
A peregrine falcon appeared for each shoulder
as I cleared the road with a broken shovel,
I buried your horses also, under a freesia wreath.
Winter cried like a bell in the clock tower
for our return to the rest of its barrow,
although we already disappeared in a blizzard.
The gales weathered my body like a bare cliff,
I sang as the spectral air filled my mouth
with roots then the branches grew back to you,
this forest path another country for our sleep.

Blood River, Kentucky

Trees blackened the valley after the lightning fire
on the ridge I gazed at the split pines of its beginning.
I added a broken stone to the semblance of a guide pile
and departed the charred staves like incense burnt.
I placed a handful of fallen leaves inside my boots,
the sky changed with cloud and hawk like autumn
where the river enters the lake
endless after people massacred the other people,
rusted cross signs indicate transplanted ancient graves.
The cold ground sends a running deer to the archer
whose arrow whirls in the void like a hunting bird,
gesturing peace I ate meat from my provided limbs.

The Harrow Succors

Winter lay over the lake like a capsized sail,
I retreated into trees to escape the biting air
as the moon arose from wheat in a golden boat.
Timber wolves no longer haunt this country,
but I wanted the wild to gnaw from my ankles
and nourish my freedom with a warm blood.
I could not hide myself from this elusive love
hating the weakness that kept me chained
until the sky lent me darkness like a perfect armor.
The vines and thorns entwine like red sisters
I put to my lips in a bliss
as the harrow succors the trembling ground.

Over the Alder Grove

The river lured the moon's touching arms
and the night sky followed dripping silk
like amatory tapestries over the alder grove.
I left the axe-head to rest in the ground
beside a circle of stones
I am stilled and imitate
the wood's mystical body accepting the flame.
In the morning I will travel back over the road
to become another person entirely.
I am thankful for nourishment from your animal
like I gave my life for you through the grave
of our mouths threaded with sinew together
like the sewn eye of a hunting falcon opens.

The Bay Dreamt

And again the bay dreamt it was rain
moving beyond itself in impermanence,
freed to leave like brilliant tall ships
from the burnt hills of ancestral lands.
An oak grew from loose rocks on the shore
then I remembered
the wood grave I laid hidden under bark,
your spindrift hand made visible the wind
and enlivens the tree in a water of air
like the undulation of green anemone.

Land Between the Lakes

A white barge motionless in distance upon white roughs
like a floating tower as liberated winds exult on the lake,
torrents cascaded over the breakwater like a spray of iris.
A dead green buoy lay on the rocks with its rusted chain
like a giant's eye while I kicked clam shells on the beach,
I called the grey rainfall to come clothe me with your sky
and drape everywhere like another day of survival.
Silent eagles hunted the shore like a dark monolith
in their lordship, I stilled where the robes fell like shadow.
Tearing gusts carried me into abandon like a pine shelter
where I wanted to remain an instant more like waking
in the morning as sun suffered its body like a birth to rise.

The Blue Corridor

I walked the blue corridor of accepting stone,
the cool wall beside held close a towering hill
and the smooth floor beneath raised the creek
like the burdening weight of my turning year.
Then I let go of futile and hurting impatience,
but after release stillness became my enemy,
a knife ignited fire in the kindling of my wrist,
reborn I saw the silhouetting of a golden eagle.

The Railing

Hills tilted into the river
like glistening shields,
I piloted into the sun wash
turned mother-of-pearl
against the wind of evening.
The boats glowed white
as the movements of horses
then stilled without notice
like beauty,
I vaulted from the railing.
Submerged in quiet water
like release from my being
alone as we are,
I found myself in the down
like the chair of our bodies
set alike to receive each
in its given place prepared
for feast or sleep.
I grieved for all leaving
touched in understanding
as we trailed in the wake.

Where Valleys Fell

Pines trees walked
with the rainy river
on a blue farm.
I retained
the contour blur
where valleys fell
like a thief
of continuum.
I gave the hatred
and disdain
for the fled
to an intimate friend,
sometimes a guard
from the weathers
and wash endured
despite a seal
over real knowing.
Branches protected
gently like the brim
of my slouch hat.

Rose Window

She kneels toward her origin
climbing sun shafts of rose light
into her own body of sky.
The aching of cathedrals breaks
at the neck of her summer dress
while we rejoice for a moment
tearing us close in the dark earth.
Locked forever in another's flesh
I wear born the ghost shadow
she left warm on my mouth
for the ash burnt on ashes
also forms an empress crown.

Ladder of Arrows

At last the low grey hawk
left shadows on the grasses
before the opening of stone
for the ghost procession.
I stepped into the intervals
of air alive in resistance
like a hiatus
when the wind moved
rippling over me like the creek.
I put moss and red splinters
into my mouth like a risk
when I loved this presence
existing to thrill and change.
I climbed a ladder of arrows
from night water to the sky.

Scattering of Migrations

At scattering of migrations
these blue movements flood
as every bird becomes the sky
and every fish becomes a wave.
We rain
lit into the unceasing horizon
where sunset halves the world
in silhouette of man and woman
to marry in silver
like a gannet diving to water
through its own white body
in a bright sublimation.

The Shelter Wood

Ending ten nights
on blue tile and sarissa,
I crushed rosemary
to my face
sitting in a circle
under the shelter wood.
Thrilled to enter
the darkness again,
I was altered
like my finest garment
to become right
and unneeding redress.
The new moon rested half
in the black cover
I drew to conclude
a hiding into the other,
I mistook the silence
for the voice you gave
to prey devoured.

Queen Anne's Lace

The crippled plow rusts
in the tall grass
of the vacant manor grounds
flooded by spring rains.
Frogs plunge from the twigs
muddying the creek,
I was glad
that my reflection vanished.
No one else was around
to confuse my quiet blurred
into yours to become unreal
like the Queen Anne's Lace sways.
I slept to be reborn
among the pulled roots
of wild carrots
covering the sun ditch.

Sun Purified

Come to me,
sun purified
through the feathers
of a soaring osprey
like a nimbus circle.
I am servant
to the journey
of quiet gods.

Epitaph Seven Years Past

Morning glories open the field
like snow glistening in sun,
this light tangled in vines
again refuses my entrance here.
I turn the loose earth
searching murmurs for the presence
of animal steps
wild behind the shadow of a queen
offering figs
from her milky sycamore arms.
Legend then I held you
for the forest transforming
as if we were alive
while the world like a cenotaph
disguises our closeness with sky.

Biography

John Swain lives in Louisville, Kentucky. *Ring the Sycamore Sky* is his first collection.

2014 Releases

Visit Red Paint Hill Publishing
for submission guidelines, author interviews, to purchase
books & to receive announcements.
www.redpainthill.com

**"This city is a lady with a littered heart
and a drunken locksmith for a father."**

The Blackbird Spirituals poems are sad bastard poems, poems about longing, poems about place, and being misplaced. Treadway opens his guts and pours them into a finely tuned book of poems and postcards.

Treadway is a Kentucky mystic. Singing old harp hymns and casting chicken bones on a plank floor. In *The Blackbird Spirituals* he takes that seer's eye and trains it on Portland and tells it like it is in a voice as universal as... the gospel itself: Heavy enough so that the best-read intellectual can drink his fill, and simple enough so that the small child can dip down and take a drink of water. It's the roar of the Pacific Ocean and the whisper of mountain streams. It's full emersion and infant baptism. It's the Lion of the Tribe of Judah and a lamb that was slain. Reading *The Blackbird Spirituals* is like church, or like how church was always supposed to be.

– Verless Doran, American poet

Siblings is the 2013 DIAGRAM Innovative Fiction Contest winner, selected by judge Ben Marcus, who had this to say about the story:

Suzanne Burns has perfectly captured the powerful strangeness of childhood, the fear and joy and weird rituals we invent to work out our place in the world. She is a visionary poet, with an imagination I'd kill for, and in *Siblings* she's written a piece of otherworldly, mythic sorrow.

Get ready to blast through the haunted back alleys and front doors of the past. Powerful, inimitable, and unforgettable!

—Meg Tuite

Also available at
Powell's Books
1005 W Burnside St.
Portland, OR 97209
503-228-4651
9:00 a.m. - 11:00 p.m.

Windsock Etiquette is moonlight on the porches of Pennsylvania mill towns, but like Berrigan it wears its heart on its blue collar and yearns for simplicity in an age where everything seems so damned complicated. This book is love poems, death poems, songs of potential and broken promise--it takes urban culture back to nature and redefines Americana in a time when we're still very much searching for ourselves.

- John Dorsey, American poet & playwright

In the same way I'm drawn to a Terrance Malick film, a Miles Davis record, an ink blot Rorschach test, I'm drawn towards *Windsock Etiquette*, the collection of linked free-form sonnets by Zach Fishel, spanning across 52 pieces without title, without pandering or any other fence posts to hang a lantern to light one's path through the verse.

This is an adventurous work, where all poems communicate with each other in a resounding way, revealing each strand heartbeat by heartbeat. It feels like a random car ride west across America, searching for gas station coffee, tuning the radio randomly and gathering clips of beautiful info.

-Bud Smith, writer, reviewer

The poems in *Mother is a Verb* reveal a very forthright study of who our mothers really are. After reflecting on the mother-relationship, I decided that we all have intensely strong thoughts about our mothers, grandmothers, or anyone else who became our mother figure. These can either be positive or negative. At some point in our lives, by pinpointing who our mother figure really is/was internally, we then can begin to understand our own flaws, our own talents, and our inner voice. Mother is not just a word, but it is movement, it is action. Mother is our future and our past. Mother….does. Mother…is.

Cover Artwork: Alexandra Eldridge

Contributors include: David Ebenbach, Jennifer Givhan, LS Bassen, Brian Bodeur, Kiley Cogis Brodeur, Alyssa Yankwitt, Hedwika Cox, Bree A Rofle, Steve Brightman, Zach Fishel, Nandini Dhar, Claudia Serea, MJ Iuppa, James Sanchez, Heather Minette, Andrea Rogers, Alicia Elkort, Tracy Davidson, Autumn Konopka, Michael Mark, Mary Lou Buschi, Laurie Jean Cannady, Nicole Caruso Garcia, Jay Sizemore, Brian Patrick Heston, Abigail Wyatt, Telaina Eriksen, Ian Spiegel-Blum

About The Autism Foundation of TN

Karen and Steve Blake founded the Autism Foundation of Tennessee to help families receive therapy and support needed at the lowest possible cost. Karen has a Master's degree in Special Education and Speech-Language Pathology. Before having a child with Autism, she worked 11 years in the public school systems in Atlanta.

After experiencing the intensive therapy and the cost associated with it, Karen realized the need for a non-profit organization to help raise money and to provide individualized programs and services for children with autism and related disorders in Tennessee. The AFT helps children of all ages and will be expanding soon to offer even more services.

The Autism Foundation of TN offers a full range of services for children and adolescents. Some of the targeted skills include: Behavior therapy, Communication, Self-help Skills, Academics, Socialization, Vocational skills, and Family and School Support. The AFT works collaboratively with school systems, and other professionals.

Services Provided:
Speech Therapy
ABA Therapy
Occupational Therapy
Training and Support

Contact info at www.autismfoundationtn.org

www.ingramcontent.com/pod-product-compliance
Lightning Source LLC
Chambersburg PA
CBHW060327050426
42449CB00011B/2690